Blessed Endings
Beautiful Beginnings

REFLECT ON JESUS
REMEMBER GOD'S FAITHFULNESS
AND RENEW YOUR SOUL
FOR THE NEW YEAR

Blessed Endings
Beautiful Beginnings

Nicki Koziarz Ministries
www.NickiKoziarz.com

TABLE OF CONTENTS FOR
Blessed Endings
Beautiful Beginnings

Start Here

I've always struggled with my relationship with God from December to January. It's such a busy season, but it also feels so commercialized. Add in the pressure to prepare your list of goals, to-do's, and everything else for the New Year, and mercy... We can just feel like this is a season to completely check out spiritually.

So, *let's do something different this year.*

Let's not put pressure on ourselves to do an advent study every week or an entire evaluation of our lives. Instead, let's spend some time studying Luke, a little bit of time reflecting on all God has done, and a little bit more time renewing our strength.

But those who trust in the Lord will find new strength. They will soar high on wings like eagles. They will run and not grow weary. They will walk and not faint.

ISAIAH 40:31 (NLT)

Start Here

So *here's the deal.*

I've made this study as simple as possible. If you are a do-it-all-at-once woman, you can take a day or two and process the whole thing. Or, if you're a little-bit-at-a-time woman, you can do this in sections.

All of the audio teachings are available on my podcast, **Lessons From the Farm.** You can access the podcast through iTunes or Spotify or go to www.nickikoziarz.com and click on the "podcast" tab. Look for episodes 122, 123, 124 and 125. I strongly recommend you to listen to the teachings before you begin the session study because they will help you prepare for the session ahead.

Each session has three sections to work through: **Reflect on Jesus**, **Remember God**, and **Renew Your Strength**. Bible study questions are woven throughout each section.

I know this season of your life is full and many things want your attention, but I'm fighting for your faith and strength in the Lord. But this is your journey and your process with God. So make the commitment here and now to complete this study. I am with you, and you got this!

Alright, let's go. It's time for your *blessed ending* of this year *and beautiful beginning* for the new year.

Much love,
Nicki Koziarz

Session
ONE

Session One

WHAT ARE BLESSED ENDINGS & BEAUTIFUL BEGINNINGS?

Begin by listening to podcast episode #122 on the *Lessons From The Farm* podcast. You can find the podcast on iTunes or Spotify or at nickikoziarz.com

NOTES FROM SESSION ONE

_____

_____

_____

_____

_____

_____

_____

_____

_____

Session One

What were the four main blessed endings, beautiful beginnings
of Luke 1?

_____

_____

_____

_____

After listening to the teaching, how would you describe your
blessed ending, beautiful beginning of this year?

_____

_____

_____

_____

What was your main takeaway from the teaching?

_____

_____

_____

_____

Reflect on Jesus

Lord,

Thank you for all you've done in my life this year. As I take the time today to pause in the midst of all my busy days, I want to hear your voice.

I surrender this process of leaning in and listening to Your voice. Help me to stay committed to this process. Help me to follow through with my obedience to this study.

You are the God of blessed endings and beautiful beginnings. Help me to end this year well and start the next with a renewed spirit.

Amen

Reflect on Jesus

READ ALL OF LUKE 1

If you need to break this down into smaller sections throughout your week, here's how I'd recommend doing it:

- [ ] Luke 1:1-25

- [ ] Luke 1:26-56

- [ ] Luke 1:57-80

Our key verse for this session is Luke 1:6, write it out in your preferred Bible version below:

_____

_____

_____

_____

Now, look up the verse in a few other versions (hint, use a reliable source like biblehub.com). What words do you notice are different?

_____

_____

_____

_____

And they were both righteous before God, walking in all the commandments and ordinances of the Lord blameless.

LUKE 1:6 (NKJV)

Reflect on Jesus

READ GENESIS 7:1

Who else is described the same way as Zechariah and Elizabeth?

_____

_____

_____

_____

Using the space below, write what it means for you to live a life of righteousness. In the _Renew Your Strength_ section of this session's study, we'll spend some time discovering how you can better live this out!

_____

_____

_____

_____

_____

_____

_____

_____

_____

_____

Reflect on Jesus

WHEN YOU ARE FINISHED READING LUKE 1 ANSWER THESE:

What do you think was the significance of John the Baptist's role in preparing the way for Jesus Christ?

_____

_____

_____

_____

_____

_____

After reading all of Luke 1, how do you see God, the Holy Spirit and Jesus in this text?

_____

_____

_____

_____

_____

_____

_____

Remember God

READ LUKE 1:8-11

What a sight this would have been. Picture it with me, a whole multitude of people, silently bowing before the Lord, while incense was burned.

READ PSALM 141:2

What does this verse describe as our incense to the Lord?

_____

_____

Is prayer hard for you? Yes or No? If yes, why is it so hard?

_____

_____

_____

_____

What do you think some of the things Zechariah would have been praying for? *(Hint, read Luke 1:13, the angel gives us a clue)*

_____

_____

_____

_____

_____

Let my prayer be set before You as incense, the lifting up of my hands as the evening sacrifice.

PSALM 141:2 (NKJV)

Remember God

READ REVELATION 5:8

I don't think Zachariah struggled to pray. This was something he was very familiar with; he probably knew how to pray for a long time, and it was something he probably enjoyed being part of. Some people just love to pray. And for others, it's hard.

I find myself somewhere in between loving to pray and finding it hard. Often I have a hard time focusing and if I am not intentional about creating space to pray, I hear myself saying a lot of "Help me, Jesus" prayers throughout the day. Not that there's anything wrong with those types of prayers, but I do believe our prayers are important to God based on what we see in Revelation 5:8.

Whose prayers does Revelation 5:8 say were the prayers of the saints?

_____

_____

While Zechariah may not have struggled to pray, he did struggle when he saw the angel appear to him. (Luke 1:12-13)

_____

_____

_____

_____

Remember God

REFLECT AND REMEMBER

As we shift to the second part of this session, *Remember God*, this part might feel challenging. But please allow your brain to think back. We're not looking at your whole life, just the past year.

On the next few pages, you'll go through each month from this last year and remember some of the most significant things from that month. Try to fill in each box.

Before you begin this, it might be helpful to scroll through all the things you posted on social media this year. Look at your camera roll and write down a few significant events. Go back through your calendar for the year and look at the things you had planned - meetings, events, everything. You could even go back and read text messages or emails from this past year.

It's important to remember some of what we've experienced this year to help us prepare for next year.

Remember God

REFLECT AND REMEMBER YOUR YEAR

Take a minute to reflect and write out at least one significant thing about each month of this past year for you.

JANUARY	FEBRUARY

MARCH	APRIL

MAY	JUNE

Take a minute and write out at least one significant thing about each month of this past year for you.

JULY	AUGUST

SEPTEMBER	OCTOBER

NOVEMBER	DECEMBER

Remember God

REFLECT AND REMEMBER

Which month was the hardest for you? Why?

_____
_____
_____
_____

Which month was the happiest for you? Why?

_____
_____
_____
_____

Which month did you feel the most challenged
spiritually? Why?

_____
_____
_____
_____
_____

Remember God

REFLECT AND REMEMBER

What were some of your biggest blessings or ways you saw God move this year?

_____
_____
_____
_____

What lessons did you learn or did you feel God was teaching you this year?

_____
_____
_____
_____

What has been your biggest area of growth over the past year? _(Your walk with the Lord, a relationship, a personal accomplishment, etc.)_

_____
_____
_____
_____
_____

Remember God

REFLECT AND REMEMBER

Are there any disappointments you are still carrying from this year?

_____

_____

_____

_____

Did you have a verse of the year? If so, write it out below. If not, get ready to pick one for next year in session four!

_____

_____

_____

_____

Did you have a word for the year? If so, what was it? If not, again, get ready to pick one in session three, it's so helpful.

_____

_____

_____

_____

Renew Your Strength

Write out Luke 1:28-30 below:

_____

_____

_____

_____

The angel tells Mary she is: highly favored, the Lord was with her and she was blessed. I imagine Mary felt a little weak in the knees as she received this assignment from the angel, Gabriel. She had questions (Luke 1:34) and she had doubts. But ultimately the Lord gave her strength through these words from Heaven.

The angel went to her and said, "Greetings, you who are highly favored! The Lord is with you." Mary was greatly troubled at his words and wondered what kind of greeting this might be. But the angel said to her, "Do not be afraid, Mary, you have found favor with God.

LUKE 1:28-30, NIV

Renew Your Strength

What does it mean to you to be favored by God?
See Ephesians 1:6

_____

_____

_____

_____

How do you know God is with you?
See Matthew 28:20

_____

_____

_____

_____

Do you believe you are blessed, even in your weakness?
See Ephesians 1:3

_____

_____

_____

_____

_____

_____

Renew Your Strength

READ LUKE 1:5-7

Often we go through years that make us feel like we're just tired. And it's the kind of tiredness that no Sunday afternoon nap is going to fix. It's the kind of exhaustion that going to bed an hour early doesn't resolve. And it's the kind of tiredness that makes your soul feel weak.

It's what I described on the audio teaching as: soul-tired.

Going back to Luke 1: 5-7, what do you think could have made Elizabeth feel exhausted in her soul before she found out she was pregnant?

☐   Constantly trying to get pregnant.

☐   Accepting she was too old to have a baby.

☐   Being defined as "barren."

☐   All of the above

Renew Your Strength

REFLECTING ON LUKE 1

What are some of the other situations in Luke 1 that could have made each of the people below experience a form of being soul-tired?

Zechariah

_____

_____

_____

_____

_____

_____

Mary

_____

_____

_____

_____

_____

_____

Renew Your Strength

On a scale of 1 to 10, 10 being the most soul-tired you could be, how tired are you right now?

1

What do you feel is making you soul-tired?

2

Do you see any solution to the things making you feel this way? Yes or No?

3

Renew Your Strength

Going back to the description you gave of what it means for you to live a life of righteousness, what are the obstacles making you feel tired as it's connected to that?

(Ex: *I believe living a righteous life means spending time reading my Bible each day but I keep waking up late.*)

OBSTACLE

OBSTACLE

Now that you've identified some of the obstacles you have, what are the solutions you can implement?

SOLUTION

Renew Your Strength

Read Mary's Song of Praise again, Luke 1:46-55

In what ways do you see the strength of God coming through her words?

_____

_____

_____

_____

What are some of the declarations Mary makes through her song?

_____

_____

_____

_____

How would you describe Mary's blessed ending and beautiful beginning?

_____

_____

_____

_____

Final Thoughts

As we close out this session, I hope you are seeing the evidence of God's *blessed endings* and *beautiful beginnings* through your own life and the study of Luke 1. I love this connection and concept so much because it's really allowing me to see that God truly works through the ending of one thing and the beginning of the next.

Sometimes I'm moving so fast through this time of year that I miss it. But I'm grateful that this year, you and I get to do this together.

I love thinking about the story of Jesus's birth through this lens. I was so intrigued by all the things we studied about Zechariah and Elizabeth and Mary's song. I'm challenged to pray more and it was good for me to reflect on some significant events of this past year. I hope it was for you too!

Alright, just a few questions on the next page as we wrap this up. I look forward to meeting you again on the next pages of Session Two.

Final Thoughts

What are you still curious about after reading and studying
Luke 1?

_____

_____

_____

_____

_____

_____

_____

Who can you connect with to discuss these things? Make an
effort to seek out some answers to your curiosity today.

_____

_____

_____

_____

_____

_____

_____

_____

Session
TWO

Session Two

WELCOME TO SESSION 2

As we open the pages of our Bibles to Luke chapter 2, we see the absolute best *blessed ending* and *beautiful beginning* start to unfold. It is the end of the world without a Savior, and oh, **how blessed is that ending.**

And it's the *beautiful beginning* of Jesus's human ministry here on earth.

This session's audio teaching can be found by listening to podcast episode #123 on *Lessons From the Farm*. As a reminder, you can access the podcast at www.nickikoziarz.com/podcast or find it on iTunes or Spotify.

Listen to the audio teaching first and then begin your study. Also, remember, you can do this entire session at once, or break it down over a few days. I want you to do what works best for you!

Session Two

What was your main takeaway from the teaching?

_____

_____

_____

_____

_____

_____

_____

_____

What was something you learned that you didn't know before?

_____

_____

_____

_____

_____

_____

_____

_____

Session Two Notes

_____

_____

_____

_____

_____

_____

_____

_____

_____

_____

_____

_____

_____

_____

_____

Reflect on Jesus

Luke 2 is probably the most famously used Christmas passage of all time. Since I was a little girl, my dad has always read Luke 2:1-20 before we opened any presents on Christmas morning. He still does this and every year the tradition and familiarity of the story brings comfort.

But sometimes when something sounds familiar to us or we think, "Oh I've read this before," we can start to overlook a passage and check the box as done.

And so, as we begin to study this, here is a prayer to help us experience these verses in a new way:

God, open our eyes to see this text in a new way. Even though we've heard this story a dozen times, we believe you have something new to show us. Remove any distractions or preconceived notions we have about this text and let us see it in the way You need us to see it this year. Thank you for the blessed ending of the world without a Savior and the beautiful beginning of what it means to have the life of Jesus to follow. Help us to focus on this text, in Jesus' name, Amen.

Reflect on Jesus

READ LUKE 2

If you need to break this down into sections, here's how I'd recommend reading it:

☐ Luke 2:1-21

☐ Luke 2: 22-52

Write out all the ways you see Jesus represented in Luke 2:

_____

_____

_____

_____

_____

Our key verse for this session is Luke 2:19.
Write it out below:

_____

_____

_____

_____

_____

Reflect on Jesus

READ LUKE 2

One of the most important things to remember about this beautiful beginning of Jesus' life on earth is that we don't open to Luke 2 and see it for the first time. The Old Testament is filled with clues or what we would call, the prophecy of Jesus' coming.

Here are a few things that are important for us to recognize as we dive into Luke 2.

Read Gen 3:15, Isaiah 7:14, and Micah 5:2 on a website like biblehub.com. Scroll all the way to the bottom and read the commentary on these verses.

What did you discover?

_____

_____

_____

_____

_____

_____

_____

_____

_____

Reflect on Jesus

How does Genesis 3:15 reveal the coming of Jesus?

_____

_____

_____

_____

_____

_____

How does Isaiah 7:14 reveal the coming of Jesus?

_____

_____

_____

_____

_____

_____

How does Micah 5:2 reveal the coming of Jesus?

_____

_____

_____

_____

_____

Reflect on Jesus

READ DANIEL 2:44

What does it say about God's kingdom?

☐ It will be hard for it to begin.

☐ It will never be destroyed.

☐ It's the happiest place on earth.

Often when we're in a season of transition, going from here to there, it's easy to forget that everything we're experiencing on this earth is temporary. The Kingdom of God is the only thing that will last.

- In 100 years, most likely no one on this earth will know who we were.
- In 100 years, someone else will be living in our homes or on our land and have no clue who we were.
- In 100 years, the work we've done will be replaced by technology or other people.
- In 100 years, the things that are making our news headlines today will merely be a sentence or two in a history book.

Reflect on Jesus

When you look at your life and your to-do list, what is something personal to you that in 100 years won't matter? *Describe it below.*

_____

_____

_____

_____

_____

_____

_____

What are some things you believe will matter 100 years from now?

_____

_____

_____

_____

_____

_____

_____

_____

_____

_____

Reflect on Jesus

Jesus really is the only thing in our lives that will last. And I think most of us know that. The struggle is, the things that are temporary seem to fight the most for our attention.

As you reflect on your time and investment into your relationship with Jesus, write down a few things you think you did well with Him this year.

Things I Did Well With Jesus:

1 _____

2 _____

3 _____

4 _____

5 _____

Reflect on Jesus

As you think about the new year that's ahead for you, what are some ways you'd like to invest in your relationship with Jesus?

How can you invest in what will matter in 1oo years this coming year?

1 _____

2 _____

3 _____

4 _____

5 _____

Reflect on Jesus

This is a good place for us to spend some time reflecting on what our key verse, Luke 2:19, teaches us about reflecting on Jesus' birth but also what Jesus means to us today. For this next part of your study, I think it will be helpful if we study this verse from the New King James Version.

But Mary kept all these things and pondered them in her heart.

LUKE 2:19 (NKJV)

The word "kept" here means to guard something. Mary was intentionally locking in these memories of the angel appearing to her while actually holding God's Promise in her arms. I don't think she'd ever forget these incredible moments, but she needed to "guard" them in her heart for a reason.

What do you think is the difference between keeping something and guarding it?

_____

_____

_____

_____

Reflect on Jesus

Read Proverbs 4:23. What does this verse say we need to guard?

As you look back on this year, what are five things you guarded well?

1 _____

2 _____

3 _____

4 _____

5 _____

Remember God

"And the child grew and became strong, filled with wisdom. And the favor of God was upon him."
LUKE 2:40 (ESV)

According to Luke 2:40, what are three things that Jesus increased in?

_____

_____

_____

_____

Some translations use the word "grace" here instead of "favor". I often think those two words are something we mix up in our souls. For some, grace could mean a "get out of jail card." I once had a friend who had maxed out all her credit cards and asked me to pray for grace in her life. Meaning, a quick solution for her disobedience.

For some, favor feels like being God's favorite. Things "just happen" in the favor of God and we often equate favor with God as a form of favoritism from God. This isn't correct either.

In fact, the word favor here actually means "grace."

Remember God

In the Scriptures, there's two types of grace represented:

- Grace, as in the saving grace of God through salvation. (Ephesians 2:8-9)
- Grace, as in the grace or pleasure God has over our lives. (2 Corinthians 12:9–10)

How would you describe the difference between these two types of grace?

_____

_____

_____

_____

As Jesus begins his beautiful beginning of his ministry here on earth, we see in Luke 2:41-49 the first revealing of what's ahead for Mary and Joseph. And there we see it again, our key verse repeated at the end of verse 51.

What are some key points from these verses Mary needed to remember or "guard" in her heart?

_____

_____

_____

_____

Remember God

READ LUKE 2:40 AND LUKE 2:52 AGAIN

What is the difference you see in those verses? *If we read too quickly it might almost sound identical but there is one key point that is different. (Hint: it has to do with favor.)*

_____

_____

_____

_____

Ok, I'm not a fan of putting the answer directly below the question but I don't want you to miss this key point! In Luke 2:40, it says that the favor of God was upon Him. When we enter into a place of salvation with God, His favor is upon us as well. Because we become children of God. And with that comes spiritual blessings. (See Ephesians 3)

Mary is in the tension of holding in her heart this blessed ending of raising a child to a beautiful beginning of watching him grow into who he was intended to be: the Savior. Sometimes I think about how quickly our children seem to grow right before our eyes, and we don't even see it. And then one day, we're signing them up for kindergarten or filling out the college application and we see it: they've grown up.

Remember God

What do you think this was like for Mary to witness the growing up of Jesus?

_____

_____

_____

_____

_____

_____

_____

_____

_____

_____

_____

In Luke 2:52, it says that Jesus increased in favor. This reveals that there is always a place of growth in our lives with God, which we'll talk about at the end of this session. But for now, I want you to remember some of the ways you experienced God this year to help you increase. There are some questions to help get you going on the next few pages

Remember God

What were some of the sermons you remember from this year? (*Even if it's just one line from a message you heard, write it out.*)

What were the books you read that helped your faith?

What was not helpful for you spiritually this year?

Remember God

What is a prayer you prayed this year that God answered?

What is a prayer you prayed this year that you felt disappointed with God's answer?

What is an answer from God you are still waiting on?

Renew Your Soul

Once I had the opportunity to visit Bethlehem, the place where it is believed Jesus was born. One of the holy sites that made a big impact on me was the Church of the Nativity. It's the site where many archaeologists believe Jesus was born. Below the church structure are caves which could have been the place where Mary and Joseph stayed while she was in labor.

But in order to enter the site, visitors must pass through something called: *The Door of Humility*. During the crusade period of history in Israel, the door was put into place so that the holy site would not be destroyed by men on horses and/or looters.

To enter through The Door of Humility you are almost brought to your knees because of how low you have to go to enter. It is an appropriate posture to be in the place where Jesus was most likely born.

Not only is the place where Jesus was born and the way Jesus was born a very humbling place and experience but there is another example of humility represented in Luke 2.

THE DOOR OF HUMILITY AT THE CHURCH OF THE NATIVITY IN BETHLEHEM

Renew Your Soul

READ LUKE 2:8

Who did the angel of Lord appear to?

_____

_____

What did it say they were filled with?

_____

_____

In these days, shepherds were considered the lowest of the low. There's a show called *Dirty Jobs* that I occasionally like to flip on. I'm fascinated with this show because it reveals jobs in America that most people would turn their noses up at. The thing is, because so many people don't want to do these jobs, they are actually some of the best-paying jobs!

But being a shepherd wasn't just a dirty job no one wanted to do, they, in general, had a pretty rough reputation as being dishonest, unclean, and religious outcasts.

They are what I like to call: *Unlikely Candidates for God*.

Renew Your Soul

Meaning, the people and things that we often look at and think, "No way, God." But God seems to have a pattern of using the things others would deem unusable. It's true humility. We see a lot of places in Luke 2 that reveal humility.

I think almost all of our God-struggles (sin) are somehow connected to a false perception of humility. It's the way we start to think, *"I got this, I don't need accountability."* Or, *"It's not that big of a deal if I do _____."* The opposite of humility is pride and pride often convinces us we know better than God.

This is one of the reasons why God choosing to use the shepherds during this time was such a great move on His part! He is revealing to the world: "I don't want your pride, I want humility."

What if those places in your life where you have felt humility but didn't allow God to use them are the stepping stones of growth for your next year?

Let's spend some time looking a little closer at this for you personally.

Remember God

What is your personal definition of humility?

1

When is the last time you truly took a humble posture before God?

2

What were things that happened this last year that were opportunities for you to experience humility?

3

Remember God

What is your personal definition of humility?

How can you allow more humility into your life in the next year?

Final Thoughts

One of the things I've often overlooked about the first twelve years of the life of Jesus was that while he was God, in the flesh, he was also human. And he grew up as an actual human. He learned how to talk and walk and followed his earthly dad, Joseph around and grew as a carpenter.

God could have just allowed Jesus to show up on this earth as a grown man, fully capable of doing all.the.things. But part of Jesus' beautiful beginning was that God allowed Jesus to grow.

Why do you think God chose to send the Savior of the world as a baby that would have to grow up?

_____

_____

_____

_____

End of the Year Evaluation

FAITH

How did you grow in your faith in the past year?

_____

_____

_____

How can you grow in your faith in the upcoming year?

_____

_____

_____

FAMILY & FRIENDSHIPS

How did you grow in your family relationships & friendships in the past year?

_____

_____

_____

How can you grow in your family relationships & friendships in the upcoming year?

_____

_____

_____

End of the Year Evaluation

FUN & RECREATION

How did you grow in your fun & recreational time in the past year?

_____

_____

_____

How can you grow in your fun & recreational time in the upcoming year?

_____

_____

_____

FINANCES

How did you grow in your finances in the past year?

_____

_____

_____

How can you grow in your finances in the upcoming year?

_____

_____

_____

End of the Year Evaluation

FITNESS & HEALTH

How did you grow in your fitness & health in the past year?

_____

_____

_____

How can you grow in your fitness & health in the upcoming year?

_____

_____

_____

HOME & ORGANIZATION

How did you grow in this area in the past year?

_____

_____

_____

How can you grow in this are in the upcoming year?

_____

_____

_____

End of the Year Evaluation

CAREER & CALLING

How did you grow in your career and calling in the past year?

_____

_____

_____

How can you grow in your career and calling in the upcoming year?

_____

_____

_____

RHYTHMS & ROUTINES

How did you grow in your rhythms and routines in the past year?

_____

_____

_____

How can you grow in your rhythms and routines in the upcoming year?

_____

_____

_____

End of the Year Evaluation

FAITH

FAMILY & FRIENDSHIPS

RHYTHMS & ROUTINES

FUN & RECREATION

MY GOALS
RANK THEM IN ORDER OF IMPORTANCE

CAREER & CALLING

FINANCES

FITNESS & HEALTH

HOME & ORGANIZATION

End of the Year Evaluation

MY FOCUS GOAL #1:

What will it look like for you to get to the end of next year and see the tangible results of growth in this focus area? (Ex: *I want to grow in my knowledge of the Bible so I'm going to read through the entire Bible this year.*)

_____

_____

_____

_____

_____

_____

MY FOCUS GOAL #2:

What will it look like for you to get to the end of next year and see the tangible results of growth in this focus area?

_____

_____

_____

_____

_____

_____

End of the Year Evaluation

MY FOCUS GOAL #3:

What will it look like for you to get to the end of next year and see the tangible results of growth in this focus area?

_____

_____

_____

_____

_____

_____

MY FOCUS GOAL #4:

What will it look like for you to get to the end of next year and see the tangible results of growth in this focus area?

_____

_____

_____

_____

_____

_____

End of the Year Evaluation

MY FOCUS GOAL #5:

What will it look like for you to get to the end of next year and see the tangible results of growth in this focus area?

_____

_____

_____

_____

_____

MY FOCUS GOAL #6:

What will it look like for you to get to the end of next year and see the tangible results of growth in this focus area?

_____

_____

_____

_____

_____

End of the Year Evaluation

MY FOCUS GOAL #7:

What will it look like for you to get to the end of next year and see the tangible results of growth in this focus area?

_____

_____

_____

_____

_____

_____

MY FOCUS GOAL #8:

What will it look like for you to get to the end of next year and see the tangible results of growth in this focus area?

_____

_____

_____

_____

_____

_____

Final Thoughts

What were all the examples of blessed endings and beautiful beginnings you saw as you studied this session?

BLESSED ENDINGS

_____

_____

_____

_____

_____

_____

BEAUTIFUL BEGINNINGS

_____

_____

_____

_____

_____

_____

What questions do you still have about Luke 2 after finishing this session?

_____

_____

_____

Session
THREE

Session Three

WELCOME TO SESSION 3

Well, if you've made it this far, congratulations, you're halfway there! Begin this session by listening to podcast episode #124 and take some notes below.

As a reminder, you can access the podcast at www.nickikoziarz.com/podcast or find it on iTunes or Spotify.

Listen to the audio teaching first and then begin your study. Also, remember, you can do this entire session at once, or break it down over a few days. I want you to do what works best for you!

What was your main takeaway from the teaching?

_____

_____

_____

_____

_____

_____

_____

Session Three Notes

Reflect on Jesus

A PRAYER TO BEGIN YOUR STUDY

God,

Thank you for helping me create the space in my life to study Luke.

I am so grateful for the time I have to spend in your word. Help me to lean in and listen to what you want to show me as I begin this session.

God, I believe that as I seek your presence today, I will find it and you will bless me for this sacred time in my life. Speak Lord, I'm listening.

Amen

Reflect on Jesus

READ LUKE 3

If you need to break this down into sections, here's how
I'd recommend reading it:

☐ Luke 3:1-9

☐ Luke 3: 10-22

☐ Luke 3: 23-38

Our key verse for this session is Luke 3:4.
Write it out below:

_____

_____

_____

_____

Reflect on Jesus

Luke 3 is such a transitional passage in the story of Jesus. Jesus has gone from a child to a grown man. And now it's time for John the Baptist to prepare the way for what's going to come through the life of Jesus.

This is yet another example of a blessed ending. After a beautiful beginning, Jesus' childhood is over and, John the Baptist prepares the way for His purpose to be fulfilled. I hope this concept of blessed endings/beautiful beginnings is starting to stick with you as you study the Word. God always works in seasons. And the truth we can hold onto in any season that is changing is this:

Seasons come and seasons go but the faithfulness of our God always remains the same.

Luke 3 is a beautiful reflection of God's faithfulness to fulfill the prophecies of the coming of Jesus. So let's begin.

Reflect on Jesus

How old does Luke 3:23 say Jesus was as his ministry began?

☐   25

☐   40

☐   30

Interestingly, I've always thought that those who lived during Jesus' time lived for a really long time. But it turns out, the life expectancy for a man during the days of Jesus was somewhere between 35 and 40 years old.

There are a lot of varying opinions about life expectancy for us today. But most people agree that it's between 75 and 80 years old.

I know none of us can say when we're going to die and I don't think this is something we really like to think about. But it's important to remember that life here on earth does not go on forever.

Even for Jesus, as a human, there would be an ending.

Based on how old you are today and those results, what's a range of years you could still have left to live?

Does that feel like a lot or a little?

Reflect on Jesus

Most Bible scholars believe Jesus was 33 years old when he was crucified. If that's the case, a LOT of life was lived between Luke 3 and Luke 24. I think it's a good illustration of how our God is always one to do a lot with a little.

I would suspect most of you chose *a little* as your answer to the question above.

Where I sit, at the age of 43, I am a little over halfway through my life expectancy. But my mom and my grandmother both died at what is considered a young age. My mom was 63 and my grandmother was 65. My brother also died at the age of 45 so because of those circumstances, I tend to have a very sobering perspective about how short life can be here on this earth.

It's why I believe every year of our life matters so much.

And it's also why I'm incredibly passionate about helping others believe this as well.

So as we reflect on Jesus from Luke 3, let's remember how much God accomplished in his life in just three years. And in the year ahead for you, God can do a lot too. He has this supernatural ability to speed things up if that's what we need. Or, should the situation need it, slow things down. He knows what we need. So let's seek Him for what we need.

Reflect on Jesus

Do you feel like you would like God to speed things up in your life or slow them down? Describe what you feel you specifically need here:

_____

_____

_____

_____

_____

_____

_____

_____

Luke, the author of this text, shares historical facts in Luke 3:1-3. One of the reasons Bible scholars believe he included these details was so that in the future people would not argue about whether or not this story was a "myth" because it was filled with historical facts. And you can't argue with historical facts.

It's similar to how when someone tells you a story that sounds pretty unbelievable, you start to ask the basic investigative questions: who, what, where, when and why. This is also why the genealogy of Jesus was included in verses 23-38.

Reflect on Jesus

"Now Jesus Himself began His ministry at about thirty years of age, being (as was supposed) the son of Joseph,

the son of Heli

the son of Matthat, the son of Levi, the son of Melchi

the son of Janna, the son of Joseph, the son of Mattathiah

the son of Amos, the son of Nahum, the son of Esli

the son of Naggai, the son of Maath, the son of Mattathiah

the son of Semei, the son of Joseph, the son of Judah

the son of Joannas, the son of Rhesa, the son of Zerubbabel

the son of Shealtiel, the son of Neri, the son of Melchi,

the son of Addi, the son of Cosam, the son of Elmodam,

the son of Er, the son of Jose, the son of Eliezer,

the son of Jorim, the son of Matthat, the son of Levi,

the son of Simeon, the son of Judah, the son of Joseph,

the son of Jonan, the son of Eliakim, the son of Melea,

the son of Menan, the son of Mattathah, the son of Nathan,

the son of David, the son of Jesse, the son of Obed,

the son of Boaz, the son of Salmon, the son of Nahshon,

the son of Amminadab, the son of Ram, the son of Hezron,

the son of Perez, the son of Judah, the son of Jacob,

the son of Isaac, the son of Abraham, the son of Terah,

the son of Nahor, the son of Serug, the son of Reu,

the son of Peleg, the son of Eber, the son of Shelah,

the son of Cainan, the son of Arphaxad, the son of Shem

the son of Noah, the son of Lamech, the son of Methuselah,

the son of Enoch, the son of Jared, the son of Mahalalel

the son of Cainan, the son of Enosh, the son of Seth,

the son of Adam, the son of God."

LUKE 2:23-38 NIV

Reflect on Jesus

Write down any historical facts you can find in Luke 3.

_____

_____

_____

_____

_____

_____

_____

_____

Now read through the genealogy of Jesus in Luke 3:23-28 and write down any names that you recognize:

_____

_____

_____

_____

_____

_____

_____

_____

Reflect on Jesus

Tomorrow night, I'm hosting some friends for dinner, so I have a long punch list of to-do's. I'm sure you know the familiar drill of what it's like to have someone in your home; I have to vacuum, get food ready to cook, make sure the backyard is picked up from the gazillion toys our three boys have scattered out there, and my husband needs to blow the leaves off the concrete.

There are things that we do to prepare for the arrival of someone we care about.

This is exactly what John the Baptist is leading - the preparations for Jesus' arrival... During this time whenever a king or ruler would enter into a region, couriers would arrive ahead of him and urge everyone to "Clean up! Get ready! The King is passing through!" John is giving similar instructions:

As it is written in the book of the words of Isaiah the prophet: "The voice of one crying in the wilderness: 'Prepare the way of the Lord, make his paths straight.'

LUKE 3:4 (ESV)

Reflect on Jesus

Look up these other references to this verse:

☐ Isaiah 40:3-5

☐ Matthew 3:3

☐ Mark 1:3

There was a sense of urgency with John and the way he dedicated his life to preparing the way for Jesus to come. He knew that Jesus was the only one who could fill the valleys of life, level the mountains that mess with us, set crooked roads straight, and make rough roads smooth.

I often think about how little we do to prepare for Jesus to move in our lives.

As a Bible teacher, one of the great privileges I have is being able to travel to events and give in-person lessons. But when I see that something is just "another event" and that there hasn't been much prayer or planning for God to intervene, that's one of the things that grieves me about events. Most of the time I leave those events feeling like God did very little.

However, the best encounters I've had and the most amazing acts of God I've witnessed at events are the result of a leader with a pure heart, who faithfully built a prayer team, went over the details and made sure everything was ready to go. Those are the times I've seen God do so much.

Reflect on Jesus

Preparation truly proceeds God's miraculous work.

And now I'm thinking about you and me and the opportunity we have on these pages to prepare the way for Jesus to do incredible things in the year ahead. But are we willing, like John, to dedicate our lives to always prepare the way for the Lord? Do I put more effort into getting my house ready for a guest than I do for Jesus to show up?

Take a minute and stop this study to pray. Take a deep breath and allow your mind to clear.

ASK THE LORD THIS ONE QUESTION:

How do I need to prepare the way for you to move in my life and in the lives of those around me this next year?

Reflect on Jesus

Write down what you feel your soul is saying:

_____

_____

_____

_____

_____

_____

_____

_____

_____

_____

_____

_____

_____

_____

_____

_____

_____

_____

_____

_____

Reflect on Jesus

Preparation always proceeds miracles.

Check all the ways you think would be helpful for you to prepare the way for the Lord to show up in your life this next year.

☐ To pray scriptures around my home or city.

☐ To spend a few minutes each day intentionally praying about certain things.

☐ Asking others to hold me accountable so that I don't get overly busy.

☐ Attending a conference or retreat to create intentional time with the Lord.

☐ Join an in-person Bible study or start one of my own.
ending

☐ Signing up for counseling or some type of mentor/coaching.

☐ Studying the Bible more.

☐ Set my alarm for 10 minutes earlier each day to start my day in prayer.

Reflect on Jesus

What are the other things the Lord is asking you to do to prepare the way for Him?

_____

_____

_____

_____

_____

_____

_____

Read Luke 3:16. What is John saying about why he's preparing the way for Jesus?

_____

_____

_____

_____

_____

_____

_____

Remember God

There's another theme in Luke 3 that's important for us to take time to study as we prepare for our **blessed ending** of this year and **beautiful beginning** of the next year. It's the theme of repentance.

Ugh. *I know.*

So many of you just thought about turning the page and skipping this section! You can't. I mean you can, but you'll actually miss one of the greatest blessings of this study.

Write out Luke 3:9

_____

_____

_____

_____

True repentance isn't just a changed life, it's actually changed actions too.

Repentance is an action word, not a word about feelings. It means: To change one's direction.

In Luke 3:9, John the Baptist is saying when you repent there is fruit that is visible. And every tree that doesn't bring forth fruit should be cut down (action).

Remember God

What does Galatians 5:22 say the fruit of our lives should be:

_____

_____

_____

_____

_____

_____

_____

What are some areas you saw yourself going in the wrong direction this past year?

_____

_____

_____

_____

_____

_____

Remember God

How did you know you needed to change direction?

_____

_____

_____

_____

_____

_____

_____

What else do you feel needs some "directional change" in your life as you head into the next year?

_____

_____

_____

_____

_____

_____

_____

Renew Your Strength

In the podcast teaching for this session, we talked about baptism.

Have you been baptized? Yes or No?

_____

_____

If not, do you feel after studying all this you want to get baptized? If yes, what is the next step you need to take?

_____

_____

_____

_____

If you've already been baptized, write down your experience and what it was like for you.

_____

_____

_____

_____

Renew Your Strength

Read Luke 3:21. What does it say happened when Jesus was baptized?

_____

_____

_____

_____

_____

_____

_____

What were the words God said in Luke 3:22?

_____

_____

_____

_____

_____

_____

_____

Renew Your Strength

How To Pick Your Word For The Year

One of the most helpful things I've done over the last few years to help me lean into the Holy Spirit on a daily basis is to pick a word to anchor the year ahead. Some people really enjoy doing this, but others are so overwhelmed by so many options it becomes nearly impossible to pick just one word.

No matter where you find yourself on that spectrum, I really want to encourage you to follow through with the process below and pick a word. Just one. Since we will be choosing our verse for the upcoming year during the last session, it will probably have something to do with this word.

On the next page, we have some questions for you to work through to help you discern what your word is.

Renew Your Strength

What were your strongest
feelings this year?

How do you want to feel next
year?

Which of the fruits of the
Spirit did you see represented
most this year?

Which of the fruits of the
Spirit did you want to see
more represented next year?

What do you feel were some
of the words that represented
you this year?

What are the words you want
to represent you next year?

Renew Your Strength

If you could sum up this last year in a few words, what would it be?

If you could sum up your struggles this year in a few words what would it be?

What were the things you valued the most this year?

What are the things you want to value the most next year?

Think of someone who inspires you. What are the words you would use to describe them?

Think of someone you don't want to be. What are the words you would use to describe that person?

Renew Your Strength

Now, go through your responses and see if you find any words repeated, patterns or ideas that seem to keep coming to mind. **Write them in the space below:**

Take a moment to close your eyes and ask the Holy Spirit to reveal anything else about this last year He wants to remind you of. Write down anything that comes to mind below:

Ok, now that we've gotten you off the blank page with this process, it's time to pick a word. Here's a few things to remember:

☐ Choose a word that feels strong and positive.

☐ Don't overthink this. There's no word-of-the-year police. You also don't have to share this word with anyone.

☐ Your word should feel like it's going to help you stay focused on one area of your life. I wish I could help you fix your whole life this next year but honestly, that's overwhelming and impossible.

My Word for the Year

_____

Final Thoughts

What was something you learned about God in session 3?

1

What is something God is challenging you about based on this session?

2

What are the questions about the text we studied you are still asking?

3

Session
FOUR

Session Four

WELCOME TO SESSION 4!

You've made it to our final session, amazing job! And now we are heading into our fourth and final session where we will study, Luke 4:1-19. Maybe you're wondering why we're stopping with these verses specifically? Well, the entire concept for this study flowed from my own personal study time of Luke 4:16-19 which I will fully explain in the audio teaching for this session.

These verses are the mission of Jesus. And because we follow Jesus, His mission is also our mission. As we go from season to season, year to year things will change. But what I hope for you as we begin this session is that you will also grab hold of Jesus' mission and personalize it for your life for this next year.

This session's audio teaching can be found by listening to episode #125 on *Lessons From the Farm*. As a reminder, you can access the podcast at www.nickikoziarz.com/podcast or find it on iTunes or Spotify.

 Also, remember, you can do this entire session at once, or break it down over a few days. I want you to do what works best for you!

Session Four Notes

Session Four

What was your main takeaway from the teaching?

_____

_____

_____

_____

_____

_____

_____

_____

Our key verse for this session is Luke 4:8, write it out here:

_____

_____

_____

_____

_____

_____

_____

_____

_____

Reflect on Jesus

God,

Right now I am setting myself apart from the chaos and busyness of this time of year because I am desperate to hear your voice.

Please allow these last few pages of this study to give me wisdom that can only flow from You.

I need your direction and discernment in my life so let me hear your voice only.

Thank you for this opportunity to end seasons well and begin new ones with a holy expectation.

Amen.

Reflect on Jesus

READ LUKE 4:1-19

What are the things you're curious about after reading?

_____

_____

_____

_____

_____

What stuck out to you?

_____

_____

_____

_____

_____

Did you notice any patterns?

_____

_____

_____

_____

_____

Reflect on Jesus

I've always thought it was really interesting that before we would read of any miracles, signs or wonders of the life of Jesus, we would see the temptation of Jesus. And you may have read these verses and thought, "Well, this isn't very inspiring to end a year and begin the next one."

And you'd be right.

This time of year, we love to study miracles! After all, the birth of Jesus isn't a tradition we celebrate year after year, it's a remembrance of his miraculous life. But included in the early days of Jesus' preparation for ministry is this passage. And there's a very important lesson for us to learn as we study this beautiful beginning of the ministry of Jesus.

According to Luke 4:1, who led Jesus and where was he led to?

_____

_____

How many days was he there? (Luke 4:2)

_____

_____

Who was there with him?

_____

_____

Reflect on Jesus

Write out Luke 4:3:

_____

_____

While we are not Jesus, it's important for us to remember that at this point in time, Jesus was both God AND man. He was fully human. And with being a human comes all the human things like... being hungry and... being fed up with the devil.

But, what does Hebrews 4:15 say about the difference of the way he was tempted as compared to how you and I face temptation?

_____

_____

_____

_____

_____

The devil had been tormenting him for forty days and at the end of these forty days, Jesus had to put the devil in his place.

What does Jesus ultimately say to the devil in Luke 4:12?

_____

_____

Reflect on Jesus

What is an example from this past year of something you experienced that led you to "being fed up with the devil"?

_____

_____

_____

_____

_____

_____

_____

_____

_____

_____

As you look at your _blessed ending_ and _beautiful beginning_ of this year to the next, you may need to spend some time proclaiming the things Jesus proclaimed to your own soul. Some call this "preaching to yourself." But whatever you want to call it, it's going to be incredibly important as you transition from this year to the next.

So let's work on this in the following section.

Remember God

Understanding how to use Scripture as our weapon against the enemy is one of the things I've struggled with over the years. However, Amy, the wife of my former youth pastor, paid us a visit recently. Amy is a radical follower of Jesus. She and her husband Ryan sold everything they owned and they travel around the country in a camper just following wherever Jesus leads them. So because Amy lives this out, I tend to lean in and listen to her suggestions and pay attention to what she says.

And one of the things she challenged me with was my ability to declare God's Word. I felt confident in declaring God's character because I feel like I know who God is. Most likely you do too. But how often do we really anchor our daily lives in declaring God's Word?

I felt really convicted by our conversation and even more convicted when I studied Luke 4. Because this is what Jesus modeled for us.

Three times in Luke 4:1-15 the language of "it is written" is used. Let's take a closer look at this.

Remember God

Write out each of these verses:

Luke 4:4

Luke 4:8

Luke 4:12

Remember God

Anytime we see something repeated in Scripture, it's as if God is saying, "PAY ATTENTION."

As we move forward into a beautiful beginning next year, here are a few ways you can do what Jesus did and declare God's Word any time the enemy attempts to tempt you. Side note: sometimes the enemy will tempt you not only with sin but also unbelief. So here is a list of declarations, based on the Word of God you can use to "put him in his place" anytime he starts his annoying schemes with you.

Because faith comes by hearing the message (Romans 10:17) it's up to us to speak the word of God over our lives, daily.

So then faith comes by hearing, and hearing by the word of God.

ROMANS 10:17 (NKJV)

Remember God

Biblical Declarations for Your Life

1. In every situation I face I have a spirit of power, love and a sound mind. (2 Timothy 1:7)

2. God is always for me and if he is for me, no scheme of the devil can stand against me. (Romans 8:31)

3. The power of God makes me strong and courageous. (Joshua 1:7)

4. My faith sustains me, not what I see. (2 Corinthians 5:7)

5. I do not have to be afraid because my God is with me. (Isaiah 41:10)

6. I walk in child-like humility. (Matthew 18:4)

7. I exalt others. (Philippians 2:3)

8. Because of Jesus, I always walk in victory. (1 John 5:4)

9. My love for God is increasing through my daily obedience to Him. (1 John 2:3)

10. I put everything that comes through my mind through the filter of God's Word. (1 Corinthians 2:16)

Remember God

Hopefully, you have a good idea based on these suggestions of how to use the Word of God as a declaration and a weapon against the enemy.

Use the space below to write out any other Biblical declarations you'd like to have on your list this year:

_____

_____

_____

_____

_____

_____

_____

_____

_____

_____

_____

_____

_____

_____

Renew Your Strength

I really believe one of the areas the devil tempts us most in the midst of transition is to believe that what is gone is better than what is ahead. We all experienced disappointments and grief this last year. It is important that we evaluate the areas we might be tempted to write a story of discouragement as we strive for a blessed ending to this year and a beautiful beginning for next year.

What were some of the high points of your year?

_____

_____

_____

_____

_____

What were some of the disappointments?

_____

_____

_____

_____

_____

Renew Your Strength

How did you handle the highs and the lows?

_____

_____

_____

_____

_____

_____

If you're going to walk in the Spirit, you will be tempted in various ways. And the doom and gloom gospel is a temptation. But this is not who Jesus shows us He is in Luke 4.

After Jesus spends his forty days being tempted, he announces his purpose and plans. And his purpose still stands to this day: to preach the gospel, to heal the brokenhearted, to proclaim liberty to the captives, to recover the sight of the blind, and to give liberty to the oppressed.

"The Spirit of the Lord is on me,
because he has anointed me
to proclaim good news to the poor.
He has sent me to proclaim freedom for the prisoners
and recovery of sight for the blind,
to set the oppressed free,
to proclaim the year of the Lord's favor."
LUKE 4:18-19, NIV

Renew Your Strength

Use Luke 4:18-19 to help you answer these questions:

When you look around your life, who are the people in it that need the gospel?

What are the things that are breaking your heart right now? Who do you know who has a broken heart?

What are the things holding you captive?

What do you need to see about Jesus?

Renew Your Strength

After taking the time to evaluate the above questions, my next question is this ... what do you need to do about those things? Anytime God gives us a revelation about something, it releases a responsibility to actually do something.

Use the space below to write out any action steps you need to take:

_____

_____

_____

_____

_____

_____

_____

_____

_____

_____

_____

_____

_____

_____

Renew Your Strength

As we get ready to wrap up our study, one of the best ways for us to live out this message of "it is written" is by choosing to anchor the year ahead with the Word of God. Even if you've done this before, I encourage you to use the process below to allow God to breathe some fresh wind into this process for you.

How to pick a verse of the year (you may want to do this over a few days, you don't have to decide right now):

1. Pray. Obviously, this feels ... obvious. But don't just pray half-hearted through this. Get on your knees, get quiet, and come before the throne of God. Tell him you want this to be your best year, the year where He is God over every area you are tempted. And then ask him, "Lord, what is my "it is written" verse for this year?"

2. Which word did you choose for the year? (You will want your word to connect with your verse.)

_____

_____

3. What is the theme of what God is teaching you in life right now?

_____

_____

Renew Your Strength

4   What is the theme of what God is teaching you in life right now?

_____

_____

_____

_____

5   Are there any verses coming to your mind? If yes, write them out.

_____

_____

_____

_____

_____

6   If you're struggling to think of a verse, head to your favorite internet browser and type in the search box your struggle or what God is teaching you and add in "verses". Ex: verses to help overcome pride.

7   STOP and verify your verse. Don't let some random person on the internet tell you how to use a verse because people will take scripture out of context all.the.time. Go to a website like biblehub.com and look up the context, read a few commentaries, and maybe even listen to a sermon or two on your verse.

My Verse for the Year

Final Thoughts

While we only tapped into a small section of Luke 4, we can still clearly see the *blessed ending* of an earth without the ministry of Jesus to an earth full of the *beautiful beginning* ministry, purpose and teachings of Jesus. Luke 4 goes on to show us that Jesus really does become everything he said he would be. I encourage you to continue reading Luke 4 and beyond. But for the purposes of this study, we're at the end.

However, the end is just the beginning.

Because as you begin to make plans and preparations for the next year, there are still some things I'd like you to do. I want you to head into this new year as strong as possible. So take these next few pages as bonus pages, do them as you'd like.

I think you've done a lot of good soul work over the course of these last four sessions and I believe you're ready to face all that's ahead.

What are your takeaways from this study?

_____

_____

_____

_____

_____

_____

And Jesus answered him, "It is said, 'You shall not put the Lord your God to the test.'"

LUKE 4:12 (ESV)

More Resources from Nicki

If you enjoyed this Bible study, we highly recommend you check out these other studies available through Amazon!

A Woman Who Doesn't Quit (Based on Ruth)

Rachel & Leah: What Two Sisters Teach Us About Combating Comparison

Flooded: The 5 Best Decisions to Make When Life Is Hard & Doubt is Rising (Based on Noah)

Your New Now: Finding Strength & Wisdom When You Feel Stuck Where You Are (Based on Moses)

If you are interested in booking Nicki to speak at your next event, conference or retreat head to nickikoziarz.com and click on the tab "book now".

My Year

USE THESE EACH MONTH
TO HELP YOU STAY ON
TRACK FOR A BLESSED
AND BEAUTIFUL YEAR!

January

Word of the Year

Verse of the Year

How I feel about this month:

Specific prayers:

My goals for Bible study or personal time with God:

My goals for my home:

January

My goals for personal dreams:

My goals for my health and soul wellness:

What I'm looking forward to:

What God is teaching me:

What I need to do differently:

Goals that have gone well:

February

Word of the Year

Verse of the Year

How I feel about this month:

Specific prayers:

My goals for Bible study or
personal time with God:

My goals for my home:

February

My goals for personal dreams:

My goals for my health and
soul wellness:

What I'm looking forward to:

What God is teaching me:

What I need to do differently:

Goals that have gone well:

March

Word of the Year

Verse of the Year

How I feel about this month:

Specific prayers:

My goals for Bible study or
personal time with God:

My goals for my home:

March

My goals for personal dreams:

My goals for my health and soul wellness:

What I'm looking forward to:

What God is teaching me:

What I need to do differently:

Goals that have gone well:

April

Word of the Year

Verse of the Year

How I feel about this month:

Specific prayers:

My goals for Bible study or personal time with God:

My goals for my home:

April

My goals for personal dreams:

My goals for my health and soul wellness:

What I'm looking forward to:

What God is teaching me:

What I need to do differently:

Goals that have gone well:

May

Word of the Year

Verse of the Year

How I feel about this month:

Specific prayers:

My goals for Bible study or personal time with God:

My goals for my home:

My goals for personal dreams:

My goals for my health and soul wellness:

What I'm looking forward to:

What God is teaching me:

What I need to do differently:

Goals that have gone well:

June

Word of the Year

Verse of the Year

How I feel about this month:

Specific prayers:

My goals for Bible study or personal time with God:

My goals for my home:

June

My goals for personal dreams:

My goals for my health and soul wellness:

What I'm looking forward to:

What God is teaching me:

What I need to do differently:

Goals that have gone well:

July

Word of the Year

Verse of the Year

How I feel about this month:

Specific prayers:

My goals for Bible study or
personal time with God:

My goals for my home:

July

My goals for personal dreams:

My goals for my health and soul wellness:

What I'm looking forward to:

What God is teaching me:

What I need to do differently:

Goals that have gone well:

August

Word of the Year

Verse of the Year

How I feel about this month:

Specific prayers:

My goals for Bible study or personal time with God:

My goals for my home:

August

My goals for personal dreams:

My goals for my health and soul wellness:

What I'm looking forward to:

What God is teaching me:

What I need to do differently:

Goals that have gone well:

September

Word of the Year

Verse of the Year

How I feel about this month:

Specific prayers:

My goals for Bible study or personal time with God:

My goals for my home:

September

My goals for personal dreams:

My goals for my health and soul wellness:

What I'm looking forward to:

What God is teaching me:

What I need to do differently:

Goals that have gone well:

October

Word of the Year

Verse of the Year

How I feel about this month:

Specific prayers:

My goals for Bible study or personal time with God:

My goals for my home:

October

My goals for personal dreams:

My goals for my health and soul wellness:

What I'm looking forward to:

What God is teaching me:

What I need to do differently:

Goals that have gone well:

November

Word of the Year

Verse of the Year

How I feel about this month:

Specific prayers:

My goals for Bible study or
personal time with God:

My goals for my home:

November

My goals for personal dreams:

My goals for my health and soul wellness:

What I'm looking forward to:

What God is teaching me:

What I need to do differently:

Goals that have gone well:

December

Word of the Year

Verse of the Year

How I feel about this month:

Specific prayers:

My goals for Bible study or personal time with God:

My goals for my home:

December

My goals for personal dreams:

My goals for my health and soul wellness:

What I'm looking forward to:

What God is teaching me:

What I need to do differently:

Goals that have gone well:

BONUS
Worksheets

Best Practices for Each Day

There's a saying... *"Whatever is good for your soul, do that."* I feel like that's the best definition of what a good daily practice is — things that keep our souls well. Our souls need to be loved, challenged, and taken care of. One of the ways you can do this is by creating your own top five list of things you want to do every day. You are the only one who can take care of your soul and you're the only one who can put these into use every day. But I promise, the investment will be worth it!

Here are a few examples of good daily practices:

- Praying
- Exercise
- Taking a walk outside
- Listening to a sermon
- Writing
- Drinking tea
- Taking a bath
- Bible reading plan
- Asking for advice
- Bible Study
- Drinking water
- Making your bed
- Reading
- Listening to music that inspires you
- Stretching
- Researching

Best Practices for Each Day

Other new daily practices I want to start:

_____

_____

_____

_____

_____

_____

_____

_____

_____

Determine what your 5 best daily practices are going to be:

1 _____

2 _____

3 _____

4 _____

5 _____

21 Minutes to a Goal

Sometimes we overcomplicate a goal. Research has proven that if a person takes just 21 minutes a day to focus on a dream, business, or goal, they can accomplish so much. I mean, think about how much time we waste while working on things by looking at notifications on our phones or getting lost on Google.

You will need to be laser-focused on these 21 minutes. You'll be amazed at what you can get done in this short amount of time, but it's going to require some discipline and focus.

Make an effort to: let your family know not to disturb you, turn your phone completely off, close out any social media tabs or tabs you are not using on your computer and set the timer!

What steps do you need to take to be sure you protect your 21 minutes?

1 _____

2 _____

3 _____

21 Minutes to a Goal

Below is a chart to help you divide out your 21 minutes.

The goal I want to work on for 21 minutes a day is:

_____

_____

My 21 Minutes

1		11	
2		12	
3		13	
4		14	
5		15	
6		16	
7		17	
8		18	
9		19	
10		20	
		21	

21 Minutes to a Goal

If you were going to spend longer than 21 minutes, what else would you do with your time? Write your thoughts below:

_____

_____

_____

_____

_____

_____

_____

_____

_____

_____

_____

_____

_____

_____

_____

Made in United States
Orlando, FL
12 December 2023

40766550R00085